15 Oct. 2012.

THIS CARAVAGGIO

For Johnny & Grant,
with So much love,
& Gratitude to be
with you two in
Edinburgh,

Annie

This Caravaggio

born 1571, died 1610

Annie Boutelle

Printed and published by
Hedgerow Books of Levellers Press
Amherst, Massachusetts

ISBN 978-1-937146-07-8

ACKNOWLEDGMENTS

Agni : Caravaggio in Venice
American Literary Review : Caravaggio Views Giorgione's *Laura*, take 2
Colorado Review : Caravaggio Views Giorgione's *Laura*, take 3
Confrontation : Caravaggio Views Giorgione's *Laura*, take 1
Connotation Press : Fillide, Victorious Cupid, The Taking of Christ, Saint John the Baptist, Burial of Saint Lucy
Cortland Review : Medusa
Ekphrasis : The Beheading of John the Baptist
The Hudson Review : The Calling of Saint Matthew
Poet Lore : Maddalena in Estasi
Ploughshares : Luciano
Spoon River Review : Caravaggio's Mandrakes

Cover photograph, detail from *The Taking of Christ*, by Caravaggio (1571–1610), courtesy of the National Gallery of Ireland.

Images of Giorgione's *Laura*, and Caravaggio's *The Martyrdom of Saint Matthew, Saint John the Baptist (*Youth with a Ram*), Seven Works of Mercy, The Beheading of Saint John the Baptist, David with the Head of Goliath*, all courtesy of Art Resource.

Deep thanks to those who helped in the enterprise: Smith College, John Burk, Craig Felton, John Varriano, Wendy Watson, Jonathan Harr, Diana Gordon, Patricia Lee Lewis, Jeffrey Levine, Ellen Watson, and most especially my husband Will, who happily wandered the Roman streets with me. A hundred blessings on Steve Strimer of Hedgerow Books for all he has done to make this book beautiful.

Above all, gratitude to the paintings,
where Caravaggio's spirit shines.

TABLE OF CONTENTS

ROME, 1601–06

MILAN & VENICE, 1571–91

Giorgione's Laura

MICHELANGELO MERISI, 1583

He knows nipples, sex, gaunt cypress,
musk of melons, cheese molded into
round pats, mint plucked from earth.
He knows darkness and what it hides,
a warm cloak, lushness canceling fear
—there's no end to it, no way to enter
it fully, it hoards what lies at the core
—seductiveness of banished light. He
knows red wine, and what it does
for a man—muscles taut, whetted
knife, wounds and sweat. Milan's dark
alleys, the taunts and blows. He knows
plump figs, hard tiny seeds, the soft
flesh scraped from pliable skin—surely
a fig tree stood in Eden. He knows boys,
how their bodies are boats that wait
for the tide. He wants to be fierce,
hauling the world's plenty behind
him on a string. Tough, rude, crude.
Unshockable, and dazzling.

APPRENTICE

Twenty-four shimmering *scudi*, for four years' training.

Milan's cathedral floats above the squalor.

Old bread, beans, dried beef.

Unending, the work of grinding paint.

Stone floor + blanket = bed.

Sappy saints, cherubs, halos.

So decorous he could puke.

(Call him untrained, untrainable.)

When he's lucky, a portrait or two.

Or blood-red wine, card-sharps, laughter.

And the *Bravi*, boasting, slapping their swords.

A Roman gentleman, who pays for his company.

And a boy or two, trembling before him in the dark.

CARAVAGGIO IN VENICE, 1591

Dazed by light, he wants forever
to wander this city of churches,
garbage, spices, taverns, masks.
Labyrinth of bridges that dip into
more twisting alleys, more arcs
of bridge. Grey stone solid under
his feet, the one thing he knows is
there. And water slipping past him,
relentless, sloshing against the pier,
slapping the trim traghetto's hull,
reaching to lick each palazzo step—
teasing dance of approach, retreat,
and slow sliding embrace. Sex lies
behind each shutter, polishing her
nails. Or transforms into roguish
boy with buttocks of silk. His own
hard-on never flags. Here every
thing is lit with the sensual: pale
vongoli shells on a white plate,
fettucini ashimmer with oil, and
when the night throws its loose
cape over the city, torches send
gold reflections sluicing down
the glossy black of each ripple
of each nameless canal, and he
knows he is eating the dark.

CARAVAGGIO VIEWS GIORGIONE'S LAURA
[take one]

Behind her, nothing but black
primeval essence, black squared
and squared again, soaked in pitch,
charred in flame, sent surging down
to the darkest wave of the deepest
canal in the grimmest hour of
night. His skin yearns for it, refuses
distraction or comfort, as each pore
opens and absorbs. He is child
again. This black—his milk, duende,
alchemy. All that he has never
known and missed. Should he fling
himself on the dead painter's grave,
hail him as god? He wants to knife
the bastard, rip the black from the
guy's entrails, spread it thick on his
own palette. Next to this, everything
is flea—princes, *scudi*, death. He
vows to chase it, grasp its sinewy
neck, seduce, enter, marry it.

CARAVAGGIO VIEWS
GIORGIONE'S LAURA
[take two]

He wants her. Never mind she's been dead
seventy years. The solid triangle of woman,
head to waist, fills most of the frame, stands
there, her gaze set to ignore.
                          Backed by laurel
that surges around her head and shoulders,
she is no Daphne bent on avoiding the god,
but a knowing fleshy woman.
                          Pillow of cheek,
plumped lip, and a thin silk scarf that ribbons
from her head, whispers in ear, caresses her
shoulder, sliding across the bared breast
to hide below the red button of nipple.
Dressed as courtesan, her wool coat lined
with fur, it's the pairing of fur and flesh
that does it, erotic as hell—her right hand
teasing, grasping the edge of fur—about
to pull its curtain over her skin, or open
it further?
                          His eyes focus on that nipple,
the audacity of the fur, as each hair
bends or straightens—the shock of it
stiffening as he watches—and he wants
to paint like that, so those who see his
work down the long corridor of years
will sense his hand on their necks.

CARAVAGGIO VIEWS GIORGIONE'S LAURA
[take three]

He goes back
to grey-green
leaves and
implacable
dark, but
finds
instead
deceit
illusion
joke that keeps
Giorgione
laughing
in his damp
grave. "Look,"
the dead
man mutters,
"up close
and
closer—
pinpoints
of light,
dozens,
thousands,
like a night
sky, huge,

and each leaf
on its left side
shines.
How my
fine brush
relished
each
swoop,
each dip
it danced
with God.
Try that!"

WHAT CARAVAGGIO KNOWS
ABOUT GIORGIONE

Best damned painter, ever.

Skipped preparatory drawing.

Used miniscule brush strokes to create a haze.

Died, aged 33, in the Venice plague.

Painted adolescent boys.

Posed as David, holding Goliath's head.

Everything, including the violence, is sexual.

All you can know is there on the canvas.

ROME, 1592–1601

The Martyrdom of Saint Matthew

ROME DISCOVERED

The so-called holy place, abuzz
with whores, gamblers, beggars,
filth, ecstasy, loot. Has he died?
Does he dream such hugeness?
He sits crosslegged on the marble,
absorbs the space, God's eye,
that huge round hole, blank
at its center, and then the shaft
of light, arrow from heaven,
piercing and silent. A girl shushes
her squalling child, manages to wipe
its tears with a rag, hints at other
offerings. He is drunk on the light,
the sober grey walls, a symmetry
to kill for. He pushes into dim streets,
not knowing what he seeks. Piazzas
spill at his feet, palazzos rear above
him. Hundreds of bells toll the hour
as if they toll for him, the man Rome
doesn't yet know it's been waiting
for—Michelangelo Merisi, almost
twenty-one, from Caravaggio,
the one who'll change things.

FAMINE

Pandolfo
Pucci
hangs
over him
as he
paints
copies
of religious
scenes
he knows
are crap.
Meals
served
by
Pucci
are
three
courses
(lettuce
spinach
lettuce)
and
he calls
his boss
Signore
Insalata,
and quits,
heads for
the street,
alone with
his cunning.

PANDOLFO PUCCI

Bright as fireworks, a guy who exploded, with a weird
presence.

So quick and sure with his brush, figures leapt and danced
with each stroke, and his flowers trembled in your hand.

Not one I'd like to cross at night.

Sharp as a monkey, and twice the balls.

You could tell he was going some place fast, and the end would
be riches or blood.

I don't blame him for the Insalata joke—we were all hungry as
jackels. Any one of us would have killed for a bowl of beans.

But I'd like to have kept him longer in my stable. He
knew how to make a buyer open his purse.

SELF PORTRAIT AS BACCHUS

oil on canvas, 66 x 52 cm, 1593-4
Galleria Borghese, Rome

He fetches paint, brushes, mirror,
sets up in the long hospital hall
where the Prior stops by each
hour with wine and jokes. As
Bacchus was wild, so too will he
be wild, and credit the fever. He'll
hitch a ride on Giorgione's midnight
gondola—"No dark, no light. No light,
no dark." Background first, slapping
thick black onto white gesso, the thrill
of it throbs his arm.
              Grey slab of table where
two hungry yellow peaches tease
the jet-black grapes, whose leaves
slide past the canvas, reach toward
the viewer, sighing "Touch me..."
And he turns a naked shoulder, lets
the white gauze slip down his back,
arranges the dark silk sash, just so,
on the slab.
              He looks half dead, his
skin cyanotic, smile forced, grime
in the thumbnail. Squeezed between
his hands, another bunch of grapes,
shriveled and coated with mold,
and the shadow of the god's elbow
hovers over the table, threatens
to lean closer.

MARIO MINNITI

We did our own work at night.

When he was in the lousy hospital, I brought him apricots.

I was only sixteen, hardly knew where my ass was, but Sicily made me strong.

I could stand up to his black moods, the silences and insults.

And when he painted me, who would not know I was loved?

That light lingering on my skin.

I learned from him, and never fussed.

In truth, we were each selfish, two mutts bickering to survive.

THE LUTE PLAYER

oil on canvas, 94 x 119 cm, 1595-96
The Hermitage, St. Petersburg

In exchange for housing Mario and me
at the palazzo, Del Monte wants pretty
—such as no one in Rome has ever seen,
and I can dish that up.
          White iris touched
by gold light, a blushing rose, marguerites,
glass beaker—the distant window caught
forever in its reflection.
               Fruit lounge on the marble
bench, mellow pears, dark figs with attendant
leaves, and one striped cucumber, part-hid,
and prepped for action.
             The lute is ancient,
all its music locked in the wooden womb.
The model, Del Monte's favorite castrato,
Pietro Montoya. We hit it off, thanks to
his cabinet of dirty jokes. But once, when
he's off at a posh Vatican gig, Mario takes
his place.
          Add evening light slashing that
wedge of violet across the wall, then gliding
over the flushed face—and oh, my Mario,
you look like a fucking child, untouched skin,
shy dimple on chin, and lips half-parted.
The eyes, liquid with tears, wander far
from mine.
          But know—despite pretty,
and appearances, and all the Cardinal's
power—this is no bauble for a prelate,
but our pact, our contract.

SAINT FRANCIS IN ECSTASY

oil on canvas, 92.5 x 127.8 cm, c.1595-98
Wadsworth Museum, Hartford, Connecticut

He gives the cardinal what he wants—
Del Monte's own face atop the saint's brown

robe, plus Mario as apprentice angel, replete
with tenderness and clumsy wings. And it's

all so sensuous, the deliciousness of being
undone—flesh surrendered, helpless, deaf

to all commands—the saint's right eye
fluttering, while the angel's muscled arm

and knee support the weight of a body
filled with God. When has angel ever held

a man with such sweet calm? He nudges
the saint's hand toward the place God

touched—the tear in the robe, slit of skin,
line of welling red. Light pours down

on them, and everything else is wallpaper
—the shepherds' fire, distant rustle of oak

leaves, scent of those tiny immaculate
daisies—irrelevant next to the cascading

light, loving hands, soft white muslin
of the angel's blouse, his teasing sash,

with its own shimmer of celestial light,
reaching up, pleading quick release.

CARDINAL DEL MONTE

Naturally I expected the halo and the five stigmata, which he edited down to one.

What I like best is the flow of my brown robe, like an elegant river, and my shadowy toes.

Plus the angel's hands—his right wrapped loosely through my belt, his left supporting me, almost invisibly, below the heart.

You might say I got off easy—unpredictable was his middle name.

The first blood in a Caravaggio painting was mine.

I should know.

MEDUSA

oil on canvas over convex wooden shield,
diameter 55 cm, 1597-98
Uffizi Gallery, Florence

Too much pretty craves vinegar and
over-the-top ugly. Let the Cardinal pay
for such bold extremes, and let Rome
open its sleep-heavy eyes and see. Once
again, Mario howls in terror—a knack
perfected in *Boy Bitten by a Lizard*—eyes
rolling almost out of their sockets, mouth
wide and red, teeth bared, while the vipers
construct their own writhing mass—sexual
or deadly or both—a tangle that obliterates
his dark curls. And his yelling pours out
at us, and he is not a he, but Medusa
glimpsing her mirrored self in Perseus's
shield, arterial blood jetting in thick
streams from the severed neck. And we
don't know where to look—blood already
congealing, the frenzied snakes, that
mask of face pushing toward us, out
of the canvas, screaming itself awake.

FILLIDE
1598

"My tiger," I call you. "My queen."
Seventeen years, and only partly mine.
As intimate with prelates as with artists,
the strongest woman I've known. Fillide
Melandroni, name that sounds like palaces,
perfumed flowers, a star-strewn sky. How
did a snotty street kid from Siena become
Rome's most expensive courtesan? And
what won't you give me? Penetrating gaze,
lavish curls, soft breast, plus a readiness
to look the Pope himself square in the eye
and not flinch. The others are bagatelle.

I'll paint you as St. Catherine, robed in black
velvet and light, and you'll finger my sword,
reddened still, as you gaze out at viewers
to come. I'll paint you as the Magdalen
—humble Martha at your side—light
tumbling down like a waterfall and choosing
only you. And I'll paint you as Judith, at
the exact moment when Holofernes knows
his neck is being sawed through by a woman
whose competence may be in doubt, but
whose commitment is absolute. The last
images in his brain will be the voluptuous
red of his tent, pearl earring with its tiny
black bow, and your determined face.

11 SEPTEMBER 1599

Leonardo's advice to artists: "See the reactions of those condemned to death when they are led to their execution..."

Hours before dawn, Piazza Castel Sant'Angelo seethes with the curious.

Heat so appalling, spectators die.

Vendors tout fruit, water, biscuits, sweets, while the hooded Brothers of Saint John the Baptist parade before the condemned.

Beatrice Cenci, wearing her dignity, kneels and lays her head on the block.

Lucrezia Cenci—a shaking rag that has to be carried.

Giacomo Cenci—flesh torn from his body by pincers, clubbed to death, quarters of his body hung on hooks.

Lit by torches, the two women on their biers.

Flower petals settle on Beatrice's brow.

Tell me true—do you really think our man stayed home that day?

FILLIDE'S VERSION

He looked a barbarian, with that wild dark hair.

But he was, really, just a kid.

Or perhaps, more like a puppy, ignorant and mischief-filled, leaving his mark. Often a permanent scar.

Incensed when I slept with Ranuccio—"that yellow bastard."

His hygiene, frightful. He wore the same velvet doublet until it shredded. Ate with his fingers. I never once saw him wash.

His hands—in nightmares I see them—paint mired in each seam.

Sometimes I'd yell at him, "Don't touch me."

And, under it, a huge sadness—don't ask how I know.

THE CALLING OF SAINT MATTHEW

oil on canvas, 322 x 340 cm, 1599-1600
Contarelli Chapel, S. Luigi dei Francesi, Rome

He thought it was going to be about
those five fat cats round the table, their
glossy silks and velvets, extravagant
plumed hats, as they count and shuffle
the coins—a world away from the two
strangers who stumble into the room.

Or perhaps it was about the body,
miracle of flesh?—the delicious boys
clustered around Matthew, whose
muscular legs stretch under the table.
Or all those hands, soft and young, large
and wrinkled, busy pushing coins,
straightening a lorgnette, or leaning
on a shoulder for protection. And Jesus's
hand points to Matthew, and Peter's
follows—twin puppets dancing above
the fray, each finger charged
with the power of a Sistine God.

Then it slammed into him—it was
nothing else but this tiny moment
wrapped in light, the breathless time
when everything pauses, turns, slips.
And this is Matthew's chance, no need
to ponder or weigh—as the dusty
gold light sweeps down on him,
and Jesus, still pointing, knows who
will follow, turns his feet to the exit.

AS MUCH DAMNED BLOOD

Tell me I shouldn't paint so much blood,
and I'll tell you about Giordano Bruno
whose thoughts were pinned to stars,
and whose one crime was to imagine
an infinite universe where worlds spin
and dazzle. God is there, and everywhere,
in the dawn and stones, a skinny dog,
the woman with a swelling goiter in her
throat, the trembling grass, even the Pope's
pink toe, and each inch of his body
(unmentionables included). And God
was in Bruno's body, which had worn
out eight years of prison, led at dawn
to Piazza dei Fiori, stripped of clothes,
gagged, tied naked to the stake. As flame
licked his thigh, he did not cry out—how
could he cry, lips nailed shut?—and when
the priest with a crucifix pushed forward,
Bruno turned his head away. Tell me God
was not in that blood, or that fire. Tell me
God was not in my brush. Then tell me
I can use as much damn blood as I need.

BASKET OF FRUIT

oil on canvas 31 x 47 cm, 1599
Milan, Ambrosiana, Pinacoteca

Some battered leaves, a simple woven basket
that overflows with figs, red and black grapes,

an apple, peach, two pears. And everywhere
that longing to survive, to thrive, as the thin

and desperate stem rises to the right and lifts
off beyond the frame. Praise the luscious, touch

your hand to apple's worm hole. Everything
earnest, grapes jostling. Nothing on its own,

yet each one lonely. All that space and air
in a gold background that haloes the lost,

the soon-to-be-not. Water drops spill like tears
down the leaves, and what is dream, what waking?

PUPPETEER

I set it up so each has a front-row seat,
as close to the action as I can squeeze

them, no need for opera glasses. That
way, subliminally, they feel privilege.

Above all, they must be complicit.
I throw riot and confusion at them,

figures jammed together in a room
of dark frenzy, and I flood light

down on discrete body parts—
long naked haunch—hand extended

in horror, its fingers splayed—or
delicate foot hovering white over

the pool of water. It is essential
that each body part be anonymous.

Like donkeys, they amble into it,
sense they must work to piece it

together, each offering his ounce
of order to my chaos, connecting

hand to owner, or foot to leg. When
they contribute, then they admire.

MARTYRDOM OF SAINT MATTHEW

oil on canvas, 323 x 343 cm, 1599-1600
Contarelli Chapel, S. Luigi dei Francesi, Rome

I wanted it to stun, to siphon off
the breath, to have so much going
on, in the dark and slanting light,
that you would abandon all thought
of seeing it whole—mad jumble of
flesh, fabric, fear.

                I wanted you as
winded and helpless as Matthew
on his back, flat on the slab, looking
up at death. I wanted you as terrified
as the acolyte's silent scream echoing
and echoing in the packed space.

                        As
intent as the almost-nude assassin
who grasps the saint's wrist and readies
to plunge in his sword.

                I wanted nothing
that wasn't turbulent and dangerous,
including the angel—too young to have
learned how to fly, leaning down from
his fragile cloud.

                I used so much red
in the ground that all the hands—
including the saint's and the angel's,
including mine as I look back over
my shoulder and attempt to run—
are tinged with blood.

                This is the first
time I let myself be part of the crowd.
As each struggles to flee, we know
we're locked here forever.

VIOLATING THE PRESCRIBED

The Conversion of St. Paul,
oil on canvas, 230 x 175 cm, 1600-01
Cerasi Chapel, S. Maria del Popolo, Rome

Let's just say it might not have been
entirely accidental that in both my
commissions for Santa Maria del Popolo
I created one huge form that shoves its
arse at the viewer and makes Annibale
Carracci's Virgin and her cliché cupids,
in the space next to mine, look like
simpering nitwits. I knew I was
violating the prescribed agenda
for artists—"The rear parts of horses
and other animals are never seen
frontally, but placed behind, as
a part unworthy to be seen." But
I also knew the magnet pull of such
unworthy parts, and the horse's cleft
buttocks make Paul, flattened on the
ground, considerably more attractive.

MARIO GONE

my buttress,
sidekick,
fellow
artist, old
melon,
drinking
buddy,
my glove,
nurse,
confessor,
model,
friend,
what makes
you want
to "live more
quietly" and
when was quiet
something
to be
chased?
Never,

can she be
beautiful
enough.
In one
scale I
place all
you gave.
In the other,
all you'll take,
not to
mention
marry.
They
come
out
even.

ENVY

Dope, dolt, ditz, what else but idiot—
not to have recognized he can't just
walk away from those saints, each

helpless as a beetle on its back. Paul,
Matthew, Peter, are they not part
of the nightmare?—sweat rivers

down his forehead and his frantic
armpits. Cheap wine ripples
his skull and rattles him awake.

What can cure the sluggish
bowel, knife pain in the belly,
his dejected balls? Food tastes

like suet. He envies the wild pigs
rooting garbage on the street, energetic
in their random snufflings. His black

cape wraps itself round him, binds him
to sorrow. He locks the door, fills his throat
with brandy and swallows quick. Something

pushes heavy, down on him. A ghost, a god?
You are too weak to paint. Its stench fills
him. *You know you'll never paint again.*

ROME, 1601–06
Saint John the Baptist

CECCO FOUND

He finds me in—where else?—Piazza Navona,
and he's lost his old model, and I am selling
myself—as every newcomer, in this eternally
corrupt city, sells his body or other items—
for protection, a meal, a mattress, or some
thing to do in a boring winter. His black
poodle sniffs me out from under the stained
sackcloth and nuzzles my chin. And the man
kneels, touches my cheek with his hard filthy
palm, touches it as if I were fragile and might
break or melt. And I grin, and he says he will
paint my laughing face and all Rome will bow
down and gaze at me, and the huge tears race
down his cheek, persistent, and I know I'm his.

EXCHANGE

Lucky to be rescued by a boy from Bergamo,
with Lombard shit still fragrant in his hair.

The new apprentice, ready to be angel, saint,
or Cupid offering his body up to those

who lust. We come to a reasonable deal.
He'll learn my secrets. The essential prepping

of the canvas. Those wild arcs of incision,
as the butt end of brush slashes a composition

into the imprimatura. The room darkened, its
shaft of light swinging down from upper left.

Models bribed with what we scrabble together—
cheese, beer, tossed coins, a sugared compliment

—anything to keep them close. And in exchange,
I'll feed him, no more, no less, than I feed myself

—and I'll pour him wine, voluptuously, so we can
both be mellow, and I'll hold him in the dark.

He'll be the boy I was once, but luckier.
And when I touch him, when I hurt him,

when he cries out, he'll know it is I who
cry out, through him—and the noise

we make belongs to the wind that sweeps
over Lombardy, and does not stop.

VICTORIOUS CUPID

oil on canvas, 156 x 113 cm,1601-02
Staatliche Museeen, Berlin

For the distinguished and discreet
banker, nothing is impossible, so I
offer what will shock and charm
—seduction of viewer by the dazzling
twelve-year-old who gathers all the light
to his sweet flesh.
                    Unabashed Cecco,
bald-ass-naked, with stagey wings, clutches
his arrows and prances over the welter
of objects tossed at his feet: violin, crown
and laurel wreath, astronomical globe,
sea of white linen. Then black and glowing
cuirass (could this be a pun?).
                    I threw in tons
of V's to honor my patron—the huge one
on the sheet music, the wide inverted V
of Cupid's parted legs, the wedge of linen
that points V-like straight to his childlike
dick with its pink tip, the V of his left
leg, twisted coyly back and resting
on the marble bench.
                    I wanted him
mischievous, cheeky, unafraid, offering
his whole bold self to the viewer. (The hand
behind his back points to his buttocks.)

                                        I wanted
him naughty and hot, cheek and lip flushed
—even his toes, his knee and nipple, all eager,
reddening. And the true sexual moment
happens as the dark tip of a wing slides over
his bare leg, and feather and flesh conjoin.

Let the sophisticated Romans fall, one
by one, under the rough spell of this boy
of the streets, reckless, gorgeous, mine.

CARAVAGGIO'S MANDRAKE

I try to sneak it in—as signature,
seal, my personal avatar—delicious,
dark, fleshy as hell, the thick leaves
pushing out and up and gone. It drags

along its own fetid stink, its shrieking
roots, its fame as the one botanical
that flourishes under the gallows,
fed lavishly on semen of the hanged.

Clearly, my sort of plant. Both
aphrodisiac and sleeping potion,
flagrant as Cleopatra, a known user—
"Give me to drink Mandragora

that I might sleep out this great gap
of time my Antony is away." What
mischief to plant it next to Saint
Francis's humble brown habit, or

let it brush the hem of the Virgin's
coral robe. Or, my boldest moment,
the *Entombment of Christ*, when
his grey-blue hand dangles

over it? At the close of day, John
the Baptist triumphs—nude boy
with ram, as leaves caress his knee
—or sulky teenager, two huge

flamboyant mandrakes at his feet—
or sleepy petulant one, whose staff
pierces the plant's heart, as casually,
as ignorantly, as it pierced mine.

SAINT JOHN THE BAPTIST

oil on canvas, 129 x 95 cm, 1602
Pinacoteca Capitolina, Rome

Sensual and yes, loving, this close
embrace between Cecco and the ram

whose curled rippling horn leans
on the naked boy's wrist and leads

our eyes back to his ruddy cheek,
spiraling curls, the proud eager

smile. He looks directly at us, as if
being kissed by a ram is an everyday

affair, while the ram gazes at no one
but him, and its two front legs, poised

primly together, point to the boy's
scrotum and penis. The light is

evening, lush, trees and bushes
disappear into dark—flutter

of green leaf or a twig-like stem
distracting from the tossed fabrics

—his red cloak, tumbled bed sheet,
the brown pelt on which he leans.

As his lower back and buttock touch
fur, Giorgione's ghost slides in to form

a ménage à trois, and the boy's toes
brace themselves on the forest floor.

THE TAKING OF CHRIST

oil on canvas, 133.5 x 169.5 cm, 1602
National Gallery of Ireland, Dublin

Three men huddle under the shelter
of a red cloak that can't protect, and they
know it. Their hands know too—John's
raised in panic, trying to stave off what
is coming, while the thick fingers of Judas
grasp his master's shoulder as he leans
close to deliver the kiss, or perhaps to pull
back? Jesus's hands are calm, interlaced,
surrendered. And what rules is muscle,
steel, crude force, as three soldiers,
helmeted, armored, anonymous—only
their noses show—form a disciplined
wedge that pushes, relentless, toward
Jesus. And the fourth one, onlooker,
our man at Gethsemane, raises his
tiny lantern over the surge of bodies,
his right hand lifting the lamp as gently
as a painter holds a brush, eyes ravenous.

ABSENCE OF KNOWLEDGE

He won't ever know that the painting
will travel eventually to an auction

house in chilly Edinburgh, and lodge
for many years, its value unknown,

in the Jesuit residence at 35 Leeson
Street in Dublin, where the priests

will regard it as an odd but faithful
companion, and wood smoke will

shed an amber film over its entire
surface. He can't predict that infra-

red cameras will reveal Judas's
original ear two centimeters above

his current one, and the soldier's
leather belt has been enlarged to fit

its buckle. The priming layer will be
unmasked as irregularly thin and thick,

with a gritty texture, and the red,
yellow, green, of palette scrapings.

But what he won't know will not
impact a whit on what he made.

SACRIFICE OF ISAAC

oil on canvas, 104 x 135 cm, 1603
Uffizi, Florence

The angel grabs the patriarch by the wrist,
while managing to point a slim finger
toward the ram, and Abraham's long
beard turns irritably toward the visitor
with his new orders. But it's the whetted
knife one remembers, shimmering
next to Isaac's arm, or his soft cheek
held in the vise of his father's thumb,
or the naked body that threshes and
jerks, hands pinned crudely behind
his back, and the desperate silent
roar of his open-mouthed scream,
while the village in the background
pursues its own concerns, and serene
bells in a stone tower announce
vespers, and the four cypresses still
reach to heaven, and no one knows
anything about a boy, or the golden
light settling on his arm, while his
father's billowed cloak pours blood
onto the canvas, brooks and streams,
rivers of red, currents and surging
waves, and, of course, didn't we know
all along?—it is Cecco there under
the thumb, under the knife, arms
trussed—and no one to intervene.

WAR OF WORDS

You don't want to read them.

You don't even want to know who wrote them.

I planned to make that troglodyte Baglione look ridiculous.

Sucker-up to Vatican élite.

Sloppy imitator who stole my style.

With the nerve to paint me as devil—black beard and bad teeth.

Johnny Baggage you're zilch!
Your pictures worthless
—with work like that
you'll never make a penny
to buy yourself some cloth
to make yourself some nice
little pants—you'll go about
with your arse in the air!
So take your drawings and
sketches to Andrea the grocer,
or wipe your bum with them,
or stuff them up Mao's wife's
cunt since you're not fucking
her with your big donkey dick.

Not my best work.

I'm a painter, not a poet.

But strong enough to get me sued for libel and tossed in jail.

TOR DI NONA

What I saw there I won't tell, you can torture
me and I won't tell it. Trickle of light from a
tiny window, no one could see anything,
there was nothing to see, nothing to tell.
Were there rats? I can't say, can't remember.
Were there ropes and iron bars and
manacles? I know nothing about it. Who was
I when I was there? Even that I don't know. I
thought I understood darkness, its properties
and secrets, but that fierce dark I couldn't
know, and I couldn't gauge it, probe it,
couldn't tell it. I knew nothingness only, and
then a shiver of light.

ENTOMBMENT

oil on canvas, 300 x 203 cm,1602-03
Pinacoteca Vaticana, Rome

This Jesus is burly, heavy, over two
yards long, with muscular arms, sturdy
veins in his legs, and stout black soles
of feet, nothing like my delicate
Christ in *The Taking*. And, painted
with all my skill, one huge ear that
hears nothing now.
                              Naked, apart from
loincloth and dangling winding sheet,
he's really—no shred of doubt—dead.
His hand grey. His flesh yellowed ivory
next to the reddish hue of the three
grieving Marys and the two men who
heave the corpse into position, ready
to lower into its grave.
                              The one I care
about is Nicodemus, the guy in charge,
hunched over in his rough tunic, arms
locked around the knees of Jesus.
He looks up and out, as if to ask
permission, his elbow pointing
straight at me.
                              I want to yell
"Just do it. For God's sake, let him
rest there under the slab." But John
fumbles and accidentally probes
the wound, and Mary the mother
extends a pale hand in blessing,
while Magdalen clutches her damp
handkerchief, and that's where
this day's clock must stop.

THE MODEL FOR NICODEMUS

None of us was anyone important.

And each of us could get pretty crude.

In the studio, it hurt like hell to support those legs.

And Mary Cleophas had to raise her arms for hours.

John had trouble too, hair flopping forward on his sweaty face.

Thank God for the jokes and the breaks.

We liked it when Crow, his little dog, licked our skin for the salt.

LENA'S THING

From the start, there was a thing between us,
a literal thing—the obstreperous and demanding

two-year-old kid, with a face like a cherub's
and a mouthful of mischief (no child of mine–

I want that clear). And then, the other thing,
the elusive slippery one, silky and sweet and

ours, composed of dozens of items (many
of which I couldn't even name), including

her Athenian nose, or the way her lemon-
ginger perfume could grab me by the balls,

or how she didn't give a damn what her
clients thought—an arrogance unholy,

even more menacing than mine. I loved
her curiously, the lavish breasts, tight

angle of jaw, her honed knowledge of how
to manipulate a man, her obsession with

peanuts. Plus, she would make me laugh.
Tall and serene, she was my dappled giraffe,

and I her baboon, with hairy probing fingers
and dubious habits. You might say she was

a necessary sibling. Each of us understood
what it was to scrabble hard, to flirt with

patrons, to appear intimate, yet muffle
the soul. In a place where few could

be trusted, we knew each other, in and out,
navel to anus, daybreak, to dark, to dawn.

MADONNA OF LORETO

oil on canvas, 260 x 150 cm, 1603-04,
Galleria Borghese, Rome

Not your typical Christ-child, the boy
in the woman's arms is two years old
and quite naked, as if he's just had
a long warm bath, and he seems
in command, with his fine headful
of hair and his thin almost invisible
halo. His right hand tries to grasp
the Madonna's silk sleeve—and
a tiny index finger rises in blessing.
His bare feet squirm in delight
at the presence of two pilgrims,

while their feet, aching, swollen,
thrust toward us as they kneel
at the door. Hundreds of leagues
traveled on those battered soles.

The feet most viewers covet are
those of the Madonna on the stage
of her stone doorstep—almost
disembodied, ethereal dancers—
one bare foot horizontal to the stone,
the other erect, rising above her toes.

And—surely you've guessed?—they
are Lena's feet. And her hands hold
both towel and baby, fingers pressing
lightly into his flesh. And the jet-black
hair, like a painting on a Greek vase,
is hers, plus those strong eyebrows.
And she is taller than tall, both
antique and modern, untouched
and sexual, no one's Madonna,
but Maddalena, Lena, Lena.

LENA'S BUSINESS

Just as he wasn't your everyday artist,
I wasn't your average whore. We were
nothing if not upscale. A respectable

family business, the three Antognetti
sirens: mother, sister, me. At home
in every palazzo in Rome, with

a specialty in priests and prelates.
We knew who lived the life, and
we chased after their cloaks. Known

for delivering what was necessary,
revered for our discretion. He
was my mistake. As was the child.

But he painted us both, gave us
another life: pilgrims still kneel
before us on the grey steps; my

Madonna's foot still rests, firm,
on the curling snake, the naked
Christ child's foot pressed down

on mine. He had guts, no question.
And he never bored. But that guy
was trouble, and all Rome knew it.

LUCIANO

I called the child Luciano and gave
him to my mother. I named him
light, to offset his father's wild
black curls, his eyes like coal, his
addiction to violence—artichokes
on a platter, like John the Baptist's
head, hurled at an innocent serving
boy. Sword whipped out at whisper
of a scuffle. Bandaged arm or knee,
white scar on his forehead. And
life as a volcano, nothing but ash
and fire for miles, blood in each
painting, dripped, gushing, saints
bound, crucified, or on the rack.
I refused to stay, he dared me
to leave, and his hands became
my compass, his prick my north
star, his loins my anchor. And
filth, always, part of the game.

LUCIANO REMEMBERS

Now I'm older, I think she may have loved him.

Not for who he was, but what he made.

Folk with ragged clothes, pot bellies.

Humans, not gods.

Once I danced for him.

I whirled in front of him, a dervish child.

And he clapped his hands, gave me some purple grapes.

He would never have named me light.

CARAVAGGIO'S SECRET

It's not about canvas, paint, or daring,
but emptying junk (hunger, wounds,

foolishness, the shit that collects).
Each time I have to find it, as if I'd

never seen it before, and I breathe
gently, wait for it to announce.

The boy in Lombardy saw it in bending
grass, or manure piled in the barn.

It can hide in the swallow's quick flight,
a grandfather's nose, sudden rise of hill,

or a child's soft thumb. It has a ferocious
sense of humor. Loves the stubbornness

of crones, the million creases worn
into their skin. Boys like July peaches,

smoke shimmying up, Tuscan wine,
cobbles under your feet. Belly, breast,

buttock, nipple—all the words that roll
in gutters. It's a sword craving blood.

It knows flesh, irresistible, fragile, more
precious than art. It revels in brokenness,

the way things split—fat melons, skin,
eggshells. Its fingers prickle my skull.

PUTTING PASQUALONE IN HIS PLACE

I liked hearing the thwack of my sword on his head.

Know-nothing lawyer.

Suppurating boil.

Slimy toad with bumpy skin.

And I relished the sight of his blood.

I didn't, however, hang around to get arrested.

All the man ever wanted was Lena.

And Lena is something he won't ever get.

INVENTORY OF GOODS

seized by the court when Caravaggio fled to Genoa

two brass candlesticks
one sideboard with glasses and wine flasks
two plates and knives
two salt cellars
one chopping board
three earthenware pots
two stools and one small table
one guitar
one violin
one dagger
one pair of earrings
one old belt
two swords
two hand daggers
one small broom
one mattress
one bolster
one bedstead
one pair of torn trousers
one chest with twelve books
and one ripped jacket

DEATH OF THE VIRGIN

oil on canvas, 269 x 245 cm, 1605
Musée du Louvre, Paris

Almost every model recognizable from an earlier
work. They're like family—not that different,
equally as helpless and undone, as the folk
at the last funeral you attended.

In front, the sobbing Magdalen, curled, fetus-
like, in her humble wicker chair. And, above her
on the bed, the dead Madonna in her red dress,
bare feet stiffening. One arm flung wide, hand limp,
the other hand protectively at rest on her swollen
belly, head thrown back, and the slimmest of halos
holding steady, next to her disheveled hair.

Above, the realm of the men, hunched in their
heavy cloaks. Bald pates glisten, disciples reunited
but numbed and clueless, each wanting to erect
a fence between him and what he sees.

On the highest tier, nothing that isn't red and
voluptuous, immense sea of drapery, wave upon
determined wave, pouring forth from its unseen
and inexhaustible source, all the Madonna has given
—her womb, blood, son—plus all God's grace rushing
to enfold the model, who will soon be recognized
as "some dirty whore from the brothel quarter,"
or "a courtesan that the painter loved."

And the good fathers of Santa Maria della Scala
in Trastevere will reject the painting, and offer
it to Mancini for 270 ducats, but Peter Paul
Rubens will persist and nab it for the Gonzaga
Duke of Mantua for ten ducats more.

MADONNA OF THE SERPENT

oil on canvas, 292 x 211 cm, 1606
Galleria Borghese, Rome

A swanky studio for the painting of this
one—Ruffetti's pad in Piazza Colonna,
with hordes of his chums stopping by to
see me work at—très chic—my painting
for the new St. Peter's. All of us float on
Ruffetti's famous and fine wine cellar—
artists, lawyers, models—it feels like the
Ark. But why am I helpless as the
background wall I paint, green-black and
massive, like a prison? And the murky
grey ceiling above the Christ child and his
mum, how will it entrap me farther? My
back throbs and aches, and Lena looks
delicious but way too maternal, and
Luciano is a pain, whining and squirming
and fussing. The only one I don't grow to
dislike is the model for St. Anne, ancient,
toothless, eternally patient and going
nowhere. The fake snake alone cheers me,
one of those toys that can fool you, and I
jazz up its glittering scales, its black and
quivering tongue, and I let it rampage
around so you can't help but notice, and
even Luciano, who is naked—and that
much more of a target—is a tad scared as
he and Lena set their bare feet, cautiously,
on its clever head and press down
hard.

AFTERTHOUGHTS

One thing to paint Cupid naked and frolicking in a private residence.

Yet another to paint the child Jesus in the altogether, next to Saint Anne.

With his prostitute mother egging him on.

And his tiny penis prominently displayed.

Next to its cute shadow on his thigh.

No way to ignore it, even in the dim light of St. Peter's.

On April 14 the Papal Grooms install his altarpiece.

On April 16 they order two workmen to remove it.

He is paid fifty *scudi*.

And for one hundred *scudi* the Papal Grooms sell it to Cardinal Scipione Borghese, whose Caravaggio collection is blossoming.

28 MAY, 1606

Rush of wind ruffles the laurel, whirls dust high,
sends tennis balls off track. Who owns it? Who
arms the wind? And why does it send constant
bulletins and critiques? Lead in my fingernails,
lead in belly and legs, lead in the damned bones.
So weighted, I can barely move. But the angels
are with me. On my shoulder, their steady
beating wings, air surging round them.
At the tennis courts, a tight convention
of them, needle-thin and gossiping, their
tiny voices mistaken for wind. And *How,
how, how, do you mop your brow?* Today these
wings could hurl the future at me, tuck menace
into each quill. I owe money to the yellow-livered
bastard, but damned if I'll pay. Daggers, rapiers,
swords—we're nothing if not armed. And is it not
inscribed in the stars—"Caravaggio will kill"?
Who, who, who knows you? I scold the bickering
angels, tell them there's nothing I can't paint. And
quick as lightning, obligatory blood swirls in the gutter
—justice? libation? mistake?—and Ranuccio is corpse.
But how can I be artist with no angels on my shoulder?
Tell no one—I slashed his scrotum.

LAST WORDS FOR LENA

He said he was leaving Rome.

But he'd keep painting me.

No matter where he drifted.

I'd be like a spirit, hiding in his shoe.

When he needed it, he'd take me out.

No way he could lose me.

PALIANO & NAPLES, 1606–07

Seven Works of Mercy

PALIANO

Thanks to the rich and powerful
Colonnas, applause please! I wake
to the bright clang of bells, ancient
donkeys clopping past my window,
while a fountain babbles nonsense
into the ear of anyone who crosses
the tiny village square. I treat my
wounds, thank the relevant gods
I'm alive. Tomorrow I'll set up
the easel, knowing nothing can
be harder than this, each step
leading to death or life, those
faithless twins that watch my
every move, and no escape,
even at darkest end, as all my
fucking crimes are mortal.

CECCO

A kind of sloughing off of my skin.

As if what was left was lighter.

If he'd stayed, I might have killed him.

MADDALENA IN ESTASI

oil on canvas, 106.5 x 91 cm, 1606
Rome, private collection

Old as woe, the look on her face,
head tossed back, as though a wave
had knocked her over, nose elevated
now over eye, a twisting of everything
ordinary into abandonment so sure
and complete, nothing but flesh and
fabric left to tell the tale.
                As if she had
been gutted, thrown down on the cold
slab in the market, next to the lush
scallops. Her neck bare, vulnerable.
Fingers limp.
                And the eye, in its
perch, fluttering closed, her mouth
slack and open, and what you see is
aftermath, and all that went before,
you have no way of knowing—loss,
despair, ecstasy, or all three mixed
into a sorcerer's brew of sex and
god?
                And does Caravaggio (blood
on hands, boy-seducer, murderer,
outlaw, brute) stand at his easel,
beyond the frame, barely breathing,
wiping a brush with a greasy rag,
stunned by all he remembers?

NAPOLI

City of bewildering alleys, and that vast
helpless bay that teases its dream of escape.

City of fat rats and rancid stench, bellies
swelling, guitars, peacocks, wild goats.

City of Spanish soldiers forever marching,
drumming, saluting, seducing the girls.

City of palaces, walls that can't be scaled,
delicate wines, furs, and thrilling silks.

City of corpses left unburied, abandoned
babies, knives, darkness, fleas, kittens.

City of windows propped open, neighbors
hollering—your business, our business.

City where a man can disappear, curl
up, sleep, where nothing's left to shock.

PAINTING ON THE RUN

He has to work out how to do it fast,
trusting his honed instincts, slashing
and splashing his way forward, as if
battling a jungle's rampant vines.
Adrenaline, another kind of sword
fight, one that supposedly won't kill.
Prodigal with paint, grabbing onto
whatever models he can tempt, often
laying in the heads and hands from
memory, like how he painted Lena.

SEVEN WORKS OF MERCY

oil on canvas, 387 x 256 cm, 1606-1607
Pio Monte della Misericordia, Naples

So much that is desperate in the jammed street.
He places a torch in the priest's hand so you
can't not see the naked starving beggar, his
protruding elbow bone and ribs. A girl suckles
a prisoner (her father?), who twists his head
through bars to reach the breast—a splash of milk
rests helpless on his wiry grey beard—while two
very dead feet poke out from a wooden board,
and a cripple crouches in the dark with his crutch.
But gradually, the more you look, it starts to
mellow, the light turns golden, and the deep
warm brown of the background seems to bless
the steady flame of the torch. Now you spot
that the *bravo* with the plumed hat is using
his sword to slice his mantle in two and clothe
the naked. And the robust innkeeper is taking
in another stranger, who might just be Jesus.
The priest and laborer tend, as they must,
to the corpse on the board, while Samson,
ferried surrealistically here from the Old
Testament, raises his chin and gulps down
water from an ass's jawbone. And it's then
your eye finds the top third of a canvas
that only you can see—everyone else is way
too busy with his own little problem—while
up there, in a flurry of flapping wings and
bed sheets, two naked curly-headed cherubs
lock in tight embrace, and higher still, as
if from a balcony, a young mother holds
her Christ child close, and he laughs, dazzled
by everything so familiar and so strange.

SCENARIO

Dreaming of Malta, a knightship in the Order
of Saint John (I've painted him often enough, I
feel I know the bloke), and all my blackest sins,
according to the Marchesa, will be washed away
in the Mediterranean's endless salt. I'll feed on
sardines and melons, sip sweet Maltese wine,
offer a toast to the Pope in the hope he will
pardon me. I'll keep my fly buttoned and paint
like crazy—just watch me knock their eyes out!

MALTA & SICILY, 1608–09
The Beheading of John the Baptist

MALTA

Island of skinny cats, rocks, and dust, not
a single river or stream, only suspect wells,
while a relentless sea hammers away on each
shore. He yearns for serene Venice, or Naples
with its manic energy and clogged streets.
Or any other place that can dispense with
a screaming market of African slaves,
or the prudery of St. John's knights. He
should have been here years ago, in 1565,
a surprised knight, beheaded by the Turks,
then set adrift on his own crucifix, bobbing
calmly across the harbor. Or perhaps he
might have stuffed twenty Turkish heads
into the cannon, and watched them fly.
Now he's stuck here, he must forget
the damned island, concentrate, live
for the next painting, love only his art.

BEHEADING OF SAINT JOHN THE BAPTIST

oil on canvas, 361 x 520 cm, 1608
Cathedral of Saint John, Valetta, Malta

The artist insists the canvas be the full width of the oratory,
above its modest altar. All those who enter will see it as a huge
window, framing what lies beyond—a Maltese courtyard
dominated by its massive archway—and two poor souls

leaning at the bars of their prison, straining to see. He can't
predict that an American poet, four hundred years from now,
will note "how rusty browns contribute to an atmosphere
of sorrow," and, apart from the central characters, he paints

only those rusty browns, and space, and a strange unsettling quiet.
Light, clear, bright, floods along the stretched arm of the maid,
who reaches down for the copper basin that will receive John's
head. A wrinkled woman with grey hair and black cloak—the only

one who expresses emotion—closes her eyes and covers her ears
with elegant hands, while the jailer points at the basin with his stern
finger. Bending over, the executioner grabs the dead man's
hair, clearing a path for the knife to deliver its stroke. Muscles

on his arm and back glisten as his left leg straddles John's body, his
foot pushing firmly down on the saint's scarlet robe, and honeyed
light surges along John's arm—still trussed behind his back—and
the blood that pooled from him lies close to his neck, and the artist

dips his brush into that oval of blood and offers St. John the gift of
his signature — *f. Michel A.*

80

ALOF DE WIGNACOURT'S PAGE

I had to hold Wignacourt's helmet for hours.

The painter liked to twist his face into funny shapes.

He called me Cecco

And I just stood there, looking solemn.

LIPS TO EAR

The Beheading earned me my Knighthood, and
then I messed up. I won't say how, just that I

did it in style, royally, with bells on. I knew it
would stay hidden, my deliciously unspeakable

scandal—an old rotting pumpkin stashed
in the cellar, gathering dust and attracting

mold, then collapsing in upon itself, slowly,
in the feverish dark. I knew they'd never

write it down, all their record books turning
prudish backs on disaster. And so it became

a nothingness, an airy cloud of mist, and details
of the crime would be shuffled from lips to ear,

from ear to lips, for centuries. But Saint John
continues to lie there, my rapier next to the still-

attached head, and above him the empty gigantic
space I made, where God hides in the dark and

pours compassion down on those intertwined
and helpless lives—perhaps also on mine.

MARIO REGAINED

In Siracusa, to find Mario on the dock!
Mad waving, his face alight as we dive
into each other's arms—like we're welded
together and will stay stuck.
        And he
dances round me, clapping and singing
and claiming a Sicilian does this when
a lost child is found.
        His skinny wife
with the snaggle teeth cooks up a banquet
that lasts a week—snails and pork chops,
potatoes, swordfish, salad, tomatoes, apples,
spices such as I've never tasted, and they give
me the best bed, and I see myself as a prodigal
son who deserves none of it.
                                    Mario shows me
his grand studio, introduces me to his ten
apprentices, his clients, the intellectuals
of the town, and the local Senate decides
to commission a painting.
                                    And I'm happier
than I've been since Rome—but scared
too, of this gift handed to me with such thin
wrappings I know it must shatter—I am who
I am—and not a smidgen of this feast will
last, except maybe, God willing, the painting.

BURIAL OF SAINT LUCY

oil on canvas, 408 x 300 cm, 1608
Museo di Palazzo Bellomo, Syracuse, Sicily

I allow the cold silver light to slide off the main
figures—two giant grave-diggers with monstrous
trunks of leg, sweat pouring off their muscles, close
enough for you to smell them. And while the light
hopes for nothing, it will gather you in, accidental
witness to the strange calm that cradles the corpse.
The tidy slit of her throat. Her arm still reaching
out to you beneath the arch of the diggers' legs.
Head thrown back, like Lena's in *The Death
of the Virgin*, but this face is mask, as the frosty
light touches chin, nose, brow, almost like
a ritual baptism, and I give Lucy as companion
the old grieving woman from *The Beheading
of John*—who once again will bow her head and
cover her wrinkled cheeks, but this time I let her
kneel. And I build a stone archway even larger
than the one in Malta, and let it rise until it
touches the uppermost corner of canvas, and
even the laborers look miniscule now, the corpse
tinier still, but the space that belongs to God,
not men, has room to breathe, sing, mourn.

MARIO REMEMBERS

I could see what he'd become.

Nothing like the man I knew in Rome.

All his strangeness multiplied.

Twitching, and looking over his shoulder.

Exploding at the tiniest insult.

Sleeping with his dagger.

Not caring how I felt.

RAISING OF LAZARUS

oil on canvas, 380 x 275 cm, 1608-09
Museo Regionale, Messina, Sicily

Rough tussle between the powers of death and life,
and I had to paint it twice, as the pious gentlemen
of Messina, who know crap about art, came forth
with petty critiques, and I took my dagger and
sliced the whole mess to shreds, convinced
the next would be better, and it was.

By then
my models were used to propping up a corpse.
I worked at the hospital, so there was a bunch
to choose from (some more ripe than others)
and I took care to find a pretty one with slim legs.

When I was finished with him, Lazarus seemed
to glow, his feet delicately crossed, and his arms
stretched wide like a crucifixion, one hand pointing
to the skull on the ground, the other held up
to the warmth of that strange horizontal light
that came from somewhere behind Jesus.

The light was my invention—I just made it up,
as contrast to the body that is being raised toward
the vertical. I painted the grave cloths rapidly—
striated, fluid, fizzing with light. And the crucial
moment comes as Martha's face interlocks with that
of her alive-again brother—slashes of white to suggest
his eyebrow, nose, lips, chin. Amid all the chaos,
love leaps between them, in wonder, like a river.

STALKER

Ironic that I'd once been the man in black,
with the signature velvet pants and doublet.

When I glimpse him, I see myself in an ancient
unreliable mirror. No matter when or where,

noon or midnight, he's present, sliding through
the thinnest alley, probing lemons at the market,

eyes downcast in prayer, or innocently
sipping cider on the beach. The *sine qua non*

of my every dream, occasionally in surprise-
disguise as rabbit, parrot, or withered crone,

each clad in black. (But never as crow—oh,
my lost Crow, the smartest dog that ever lived

—you'd have chewed up this fiend, this rascal,
this bothersome snake, this slice of darkness.)

And I get so I don't trust myself–when
did my judgment crumble?—and perhaps

he's a personal ghost, summoned to make
my passage to hell more hellish. Or who I

might have been, if I hadn't married my
brush. Dear determined shadow, tell me

I'm not the "foul and fetid limb" they
tossed from Malta. Teach me your art.

NAPLES & PORTO ERCOLE, 1609–10
David with the Head of Goliath

OSTERIA DEL CERRIGLIO

Back in warm dirty Naples, put
up cushily at Palazzo Cellamare—
the Marchesa (old tart that she was)
knew how to pick a palace—
I was painting like a crazed man,
as this one was for me (though I toyed
with offering it to Wignacourt as
penance for the Malta shenanigan).
And I was feeling jaunty and mellow,
happy to be striding up the stair
of the most famous Naples tavern,
and I knew the girls—plus two new
boys—would be waiting for me,
and I could almost touch them, feel
them, but what I didn't notice were
rapiers and daggers, and the four
heavies who had been waiting,
and I whacked away at them, which
saved my life, but did nothing
for the sliced ribbons of skin
that waltzed down my face, or
my canyon wounds that would take
months to heal, and I knew my
stalker had found himself some
assassinos, and there'd be no end
to it, in this life, wherever I turned.

COSTANZA COLONNA,
MARCHESA DI CARAVAGGIO

You could say I've known him since before his conception.

Forty years ago, I attended his parents' wedding.

I was only seventeen.

Never dreaming their future son would claim my protection.

Recently, more often than not.

Thank God the servants are a buffer, and can see to his wounds.

That sliced-up face, so frightful I can't bear it.

What drives a man to such excess?

I don't even like his paintings much.

Though others praise him.

DAVID WITH THE HEAD OF GOLIATH

oil on canvas, 125 x 101 cm, 1606
Galleria Borghese, Rome

I begin, as usual, with the right ear,
and Cecco's I can paint blind—red
always, softer and more sculptured
than most. I imagine that he draws
his eyebrows together, presses down
on his smooth lips, while hanging on
to the huge gourd that stands in
for Goliath's head. And, simply,
I paint Cecco as I saw him last,
my eyes lingering on his own
held-back tears—I touched, for
a final second, his hard nipple,
and knew I'd never bed him again.
Shadows linger on the ribcage,
brush the hollow where throat
and collarbone meet. Background,
a tent interior, black as hell, and
I paint his sword and white tunic
as the only glistening things within
miles. I want the scene charged
with sex—violent, but also delicate
and discreet—hence the flash

of white between his brown pants,
or the way his sleek sword points
to the groin. I wait three days for
courage to paint myself, a dangling
head that Cecco holds by the hairs—
one small lock, caught between thumb
and index finger, grazes his wrist.
And I'm crazed, ugly, desperate,
one eye flickering closed as the other
struggles to see, my mouth an open
O with gravestone teeth. Voluptuous
blood jets from the neck, as Cecco
looks and looks at the monster that
he—despite himself—helped make.

SALOME WITH THE HEAD
OF JOHN THE BAPTIST

oil on canvas, 116 x140 cm, 1609-10
Palacio Real, Madrid

Never has he painted with such a sense of stillness,
those four figures locked in the tightest of circles,

eternal black flooding the background. And we are
nowhere but there, with them, in the dark, as Salome

holds the platter with John's serene head, almost like a man
asleep, and she looks away—her eyes solemn, on the edge

of frantic—from what she has done. The old crone's face
with its thousand wrinkles gazes down as if she has been

doing this a lifetime and knows exactly how. And the young
executioner, about to leave, turns back to stare tenderly,

perhaps regretfully, at his work. They are so close to each
other, and so distant. The blazing impartial light pours

down on Salome's red cloak, her face and breast, John's
forehead and nose, the old woman's folded head-dress,

the executioner's muscular arm. And this moment
is a dream from which not one of them will waken,

they are floating in a dark that feels like mercy, and
soon they will be gone, and each one of us with them.

BACK

And it's on to Rome, as soon as I bundle the *Salome*
off to Wignacourt. Cardinal Scipione Borghese
swears he'll get me a Pope's pardon, so I'll take him,
as token thank-you, my John with the ram, and
my leaning-back John. And I can do it, really do
it—fuck all those asses who doubted I'd be back!

FADE-OUT

Birds whirl overhead in their black starry
host, while he is dragged in this creaking

ox cart to Porto Ercole, where the powerful
ones have determined he must die. His soul

bobbing behind him, kite on a string,
loath to cut the cord and let him go.

NOTES ON THE POEMS:

p. 18, *Self Portrait as Bacchus*: Caravaggio had a prolonged and somewhat mysterious illness and was cared for at Hospital of Santa Maria della Consolazione. One report claims he was wounded by a horse.

p. 20, *The Lute Player*: Cardinal del Monte (who had many friends in the arts and sciences, including Galileo) befriended Caravaggio and gave him and Mario Minniti rooms and a studio at his Palazzo Madama.

p. 24, "11 September 1599": Francesco Cenci (abuser and tyrant parent) apparently fell to his death from a balcony on his castle. It turned out he had been murdered: his daughter Beatrice, his second wife Lucrezia Cenci, and his son Giacomo were tortured, tried, and convicted.

p. 39, "Cecco Found": Cecco's real name was Francesco Buoneri. As an adult, he became a famous artist.

p. 41, "Victorious Cupid": The patron is the banker Vincenzo Guistiniani, friend and neighbor of Del Monte.

p. 48, "War of Words": Caravaggio and his friends, Onorio Longhi and Orazio Gentileschi, wrote scurrilous verses about Baglione and circulated them widely around Rome. All three were charged with libel.

p. 57, "Luciano": While it is clear that Caravaggio had a long-term relationship with Lena Antognetti, and that she had a child called Luciano, it is by no means clear that Caravaggio was the father.

p. 80, "The Beheading of St. John the Baptist": the "f." in the signature may stand for "fecit" (made) or for Frater (brother knight). Michel A refers to Michel Angelo, his original name.

The contemporary poet who notes "how rusty browns contribute to an atmosphere of sorrow" is Gregory Orr.

p. 81: "Alof de Wignacourt's Page": See Caravaggio's *Portrait of Alof de Wignacourt,* the Grand Master of the Nights of Malta.

p. 97, "Fade-Out": Caravaggio sailed from Naples. Mysteriously the boat did not stop in Civitavecchia, the port for Rome— clearly, someone must have bribed the ship's captain not to stop—but continued to Palo where he was arrested, imprisoned, and then bought his release. The official and unbelievable story is that he saw the boat, with his paintings aboard, sailing up the coast and that he ran after the boat, through malarial swamps, over one hundred kilmometers, in blazing heat, and died in Porto Ercole, a Tuscan town. No body was produced, and it is highly likely that he was murdered. What is certain is that the boat returned safely to Naples with his paintings, and Scipio Borghese ended up with more Caravaggios.

This Caravaggio was designed and printed by
Steve Strimer of Levellers Press

The paper is Mohawk Vellum
Set in Baskerville types